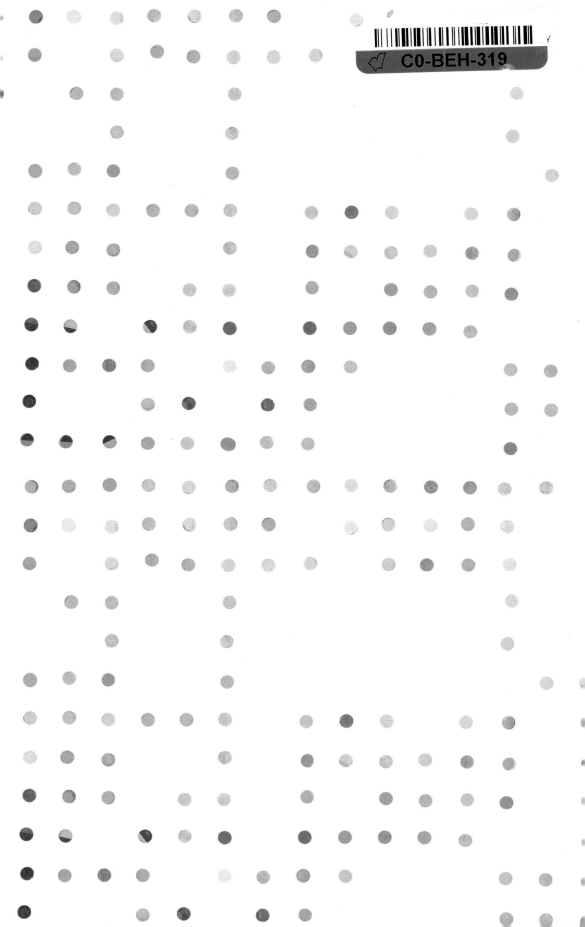

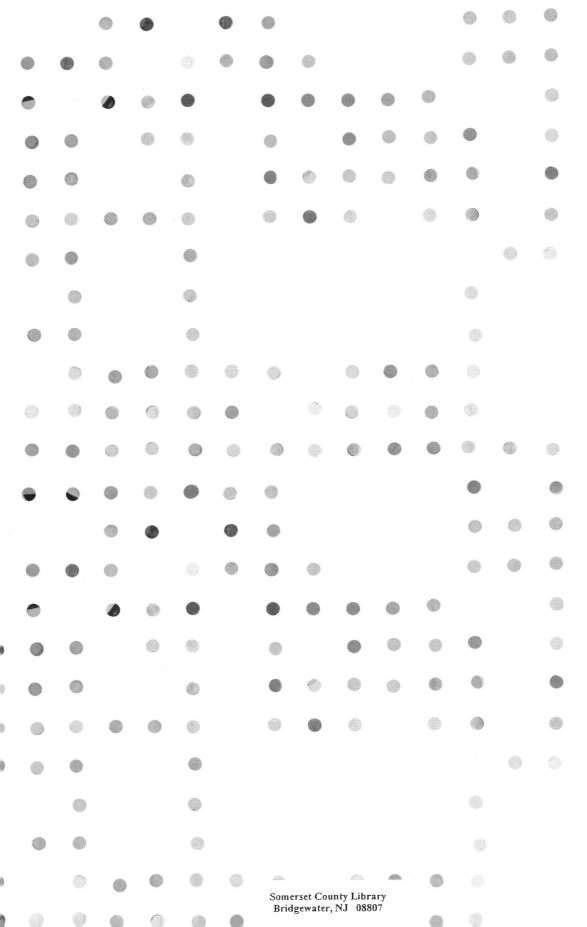

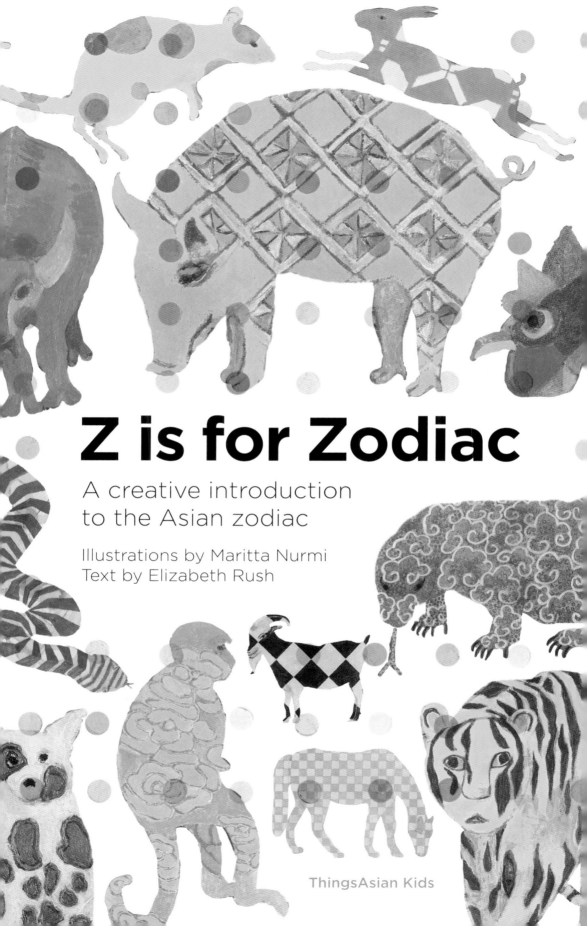

Z is for Zodiac

A creative introduction
to the Asian zodiac

Illustrations by Maritta Nurmi
Text by Elizabeth Rush

ThingsAsian Kids

Z is for Zodiac
A creative introduction to the Asian zodiac

Illustrations by Maritta Nurmi
Text by Elizabeth Rush

Art reproduction by Noi Pictures/Matthew Dakin
Book design by Janet McKelpin

ThingsAsian Press
San Francisco, California USA
www.thingsasianpress.com

Printed in Hong Kong
ISBN 13: 978-1-934159-43-9
ISBN 10: 1-934159-43-3

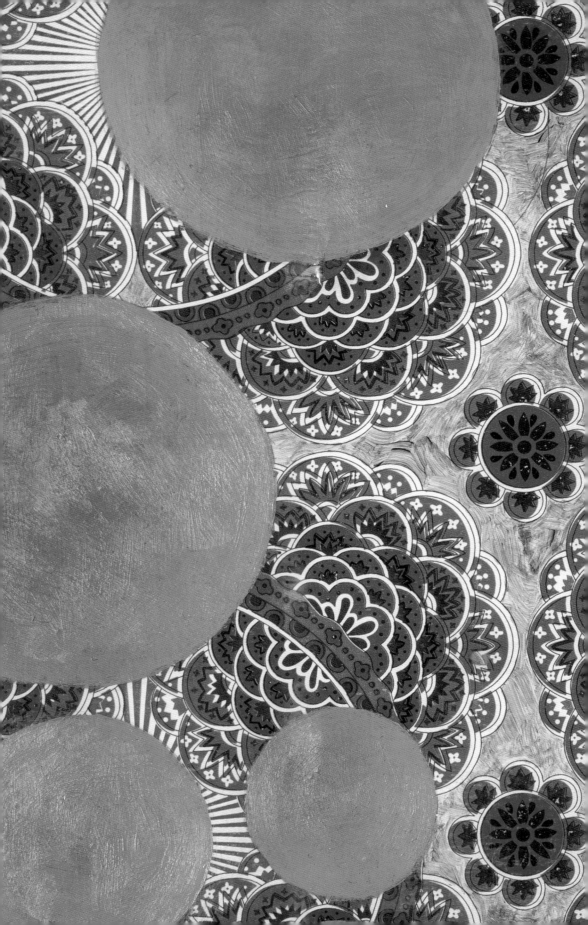

Many, many moons ago, a powerful spirit lived in the sky. Jade Emperor was her name. At the end of every winter, when the world warmed up, Jade Emperor held a fabulous party to celebrate.

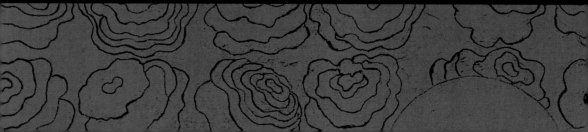

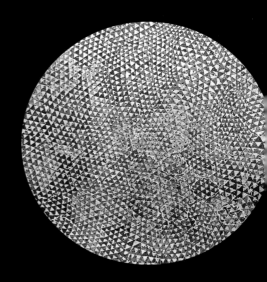

With each full moon that circled the earth, the date for the party drew closer. First the moon of the blooming apricot trees zoomed past. Then came the dragon moon, the moon of the wandering ghosts, and the heavy harvest moon.

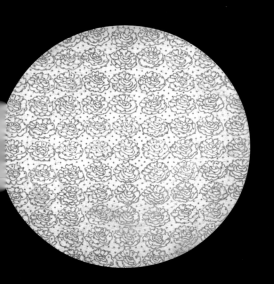
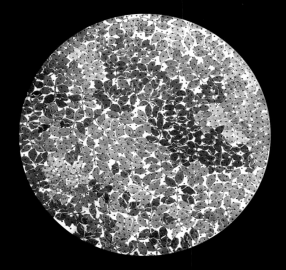

After twelve full moons cycled through, Jade Emperor knew it was
time to hold her famous New Year's fete.

Down on the earth below, there lived hundreds of animals Jade Emperor had never met. This time she would invite them too!

She would even hold a competition, naming each of the twelve years in the zodiac after each of the first twelve animals to arrive.

A roiling river separated the Jade Emperor's palace from the earth. But when the animals heard about the competition they all jumped in. The water popped and fizzed! Swished and swirled! And the animals all swam on.

The first to cross the river and enter Jade Emperor's palace was that rambunctious rapscallion, that potent rodent the rat. "From this day forward, the first year in the lunar calendar will carry your name," the Jade Emperor said.

The rat coughed and water fell out of her mouth. "Like you, those born in the **Year of the Rat** will be full of pluck and spark—fleecy and cheeky, an animal-sized exclamation mark!"

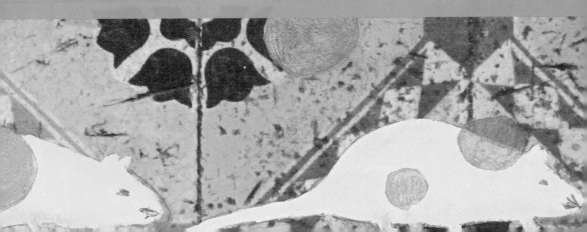

Right behind the rat, three big blue water buffalos arrived, lumbering in like a pack of purposeful pachyderms. "Peaceful and strong, those born during the **Year of the Buffalo** will be leaders before long," the Jade Emperor said.

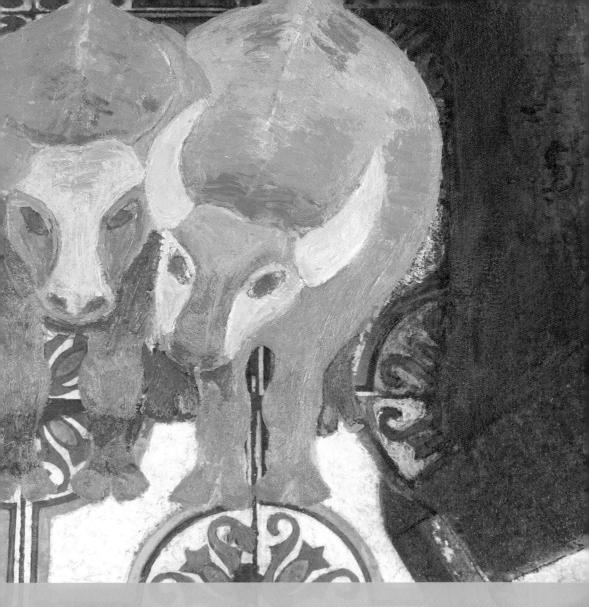

Then she shook her wild locks and gazed back into the river's roiling, wondering which animal would arrive next.

Twin tigers prowled the palace's periphery, their tensed muscles like taut ropes in a ship gone sideways. "The third year in the lunar calendar will be the **Year of the Tiger**," Jade Emperor said.

"Those born under it will be boastful and brave. Adventurers all that sometimes misbehave!"

For a small spell, no one appeared. The Jade Emperor listened to the wind swish through the bamboo. She watched the moon's many reflections shimmering on the suddenly still slack tide.

Then out of the stillness, both rabbit and cat bounded up onto the balcony.

"It is a tie!" Jade Emperor said, "So I will name this the **Year of the Rabbit** in the north and the **Year of the Cat** in the south. All born under this sign will be supple and smart. Stealthy and spry, when you jump you will always reach high."

Next to appear was that dramatic dynamo, the dragon. For a fearful second its long tongue flicked the air.

"A magical creature indeed," the Emperor eked. "Those born during the **Year of the Dragon** will be at home everywhere — under water, on the ground and in the air."

Soon two serpentine snakes slithered by, their soft bellies sliding like the blue in the sky.

"Those born under the **Year of the Snake** will speak little," the Jade Emperor said. "But every small syllable they hiss will be full of wisdom, the stuff of myths."

Over the river the sun began to rise, high up into the periwinkle sky. For a split second no one blinked or looked away. Instead they gave their thanks for another day.

Out of the sun's fiery glow, a pair of cheerful horses grow.

"Those born during this, the seventh in the cycle, will be like the horse—strong and likable," the Emperor said, returning her gaze to the river's edge.

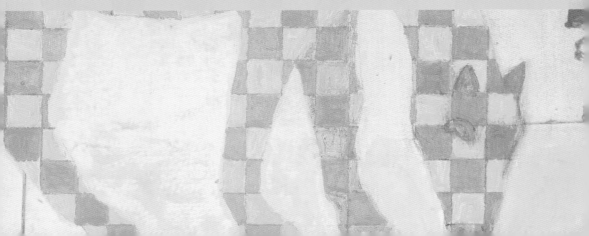

Next a gaggle of goats appeared, chomping and galomping.

When the Emperor saw them she declared, "**The Year of the Goat** will always be for those who like to eat and be free. Sidle up with one of these and you will have a friend for life, I guarantee."

And then the mischievous monkey swung in—hopping and skipping and grinning a grin.

"Many monkeys make merry from dawn until dusk—in tree tops, in sock hops, in shops and at stops," the Emperor said, "which is why those born under this moon always arrive late but never too soon."

The day was drawing to a close and soon the party would start. A hundred fat flowers floated toward those who had gathered on the shore to watch the end of the race.

The roosters' ribald call ricocheted off the palace's painted walls.

"Hi-ho! Hi-ho!" the Jade Emperor said. "Without you I would not know when to raise my head. Therefor should your birthday fall within the rooster's spin 'round our ball, yours will be a rich life indeed. With hard work you will always succeed."

Suddenly it seemed a hundred spotted dogs arrived on the scene. They lined up along the shore, like pawns in a chess game protecting the score.

"Dearest dog friends," the Jade Emperor proclaimed, "those born during your year shall never be tamed. To those that you love may you always be true, guarding the doors that all must pass through."

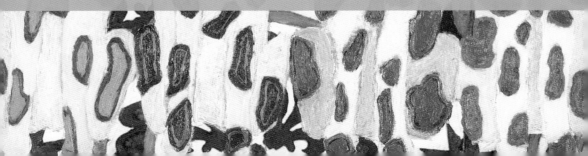

Last but not least, two wild pigs appeared, their noses all wet and their faces all smeared.

"Those born during this year will be honest and sweet, caring deeply about others without being discreet," the Jade Emperor said, throwing her hands up, at last, high overhead.

Now that each year had an animal and each animal a year, the party could start and the people all cheered. The firecrackers popped! And the music all boomed! And the hundred stone dogs took turns guarding the room.

Elizabeth Rush is the author of Rising: The Unsettling of the American Shore (Milkweed Editions, 2018) and Still Lifes from a Vanishing City: Essays and Photographs from Yangon, Myanmar (Things Asian, 2014.) She has collaborated with artists from all over Asia for the Things Asian Alphabetical World series and her essays have appeared in Harpers, Granta, Guernica, Creative Nonfiction, Orion, Le Monde Diplomatique and others. In 2016, she was awarded the Howard Foundation Fellowship by Brown University where she currently teaches courses on writing and reading literary nonfiction.

www.elizabethrush.net

Maritta Nurmi is a biologist and visual artist based in Finland and Vietnam. Experimenting and processing are key elements in her practice. When canvas is not enough, Nurmi paints atop 3D objects: mundane tables, stools or ceramic jars, all get a new beatific life by her hand. At an artist residency in Benin, Africa she added wearable art to her repertoire. Most recently she has been venturing into public art and community-based art projects. Nurmi has had museum and gallery exhibitions in Asia, Europe and the United States. Her works belong in private collections worldwide and are also housed in public collections such as those of the State of Finland, Waino Aaltonen Museum (WAM), Hameenlinna Art Museum, Aboa Vetus Museum, Prudential Tokyo and Nikko Vietnam.

www.marittanurmi.com

THINGSASIAN PRESS

Experience Asia Through the Eyes of Travelers

ThingsAsian Kids: A World of Stories

To children, the world is a multitude of stories waiting to be told. From the moment they can ask "Why," their curiosity is unquenchable and travels beyond all borders. They long to know how other children live, what they eat, what games they play. They become lost in pictures of other countries and as they gaze, their imaginations take them there. Places they learn about become part of their internal landscape and remain there, long after they grow up.

Recognizing the amazing capacity to learn that exists in childhood, ThingsAsian Kids offers nourishment for young imaginations, accompanied by facts that feed young minds. Bilingual texts and vivid illustrations provide an enticing view of other languages, other cities, other parts of the globe. Children who discover ThingsAsian Kids books learn to explore differences and celebrate diversity, while the excitement of the world unfolds before them with every turn of the page.

A knowledge and an understanding of other nations and their cultures has never been as important as it is today. ThingsAsian Kids is dedicated to making books that will help children hold the farthest corners of the world in their hands, in their minds, and in their hearts.

thingsasianpress.com/kids-books

M is for Myanmar
By Elizabeth Rush;
Illustrations by Khin Maung Myint
An English-Burmese Bilingual Book

B is for Bangkok
By Janet Brown;
Illustrations by Likit Q Kittisakdinan
An English-Thai Bilingual Book

T is for Tokyo
By Irene Akio
An English-Japanese
Bilingual Book

I is for Indonesia
By Elizabeth Rush;
Illustrations by EddiE haRA
An English-Indonesian
Bilingual Book

H is for Hanoi
By Elizabeth Rush;
Illustrations by Nghia Cuong Nguyen
An English-Vietnamese
Bilingual Book

M is for Mongolia
By Tricia Ready;
Illustrations by Turburam Sandagdorj
An English-Mongolian
Bilingual Book

H is for Hong Kong
By Tricia Morrissey;
Illustrations by Elizabeth Briel
An English-Chinese Bilingual Book

Everyday Life
By Tricia Morrissey and
Ding Sang Mak
An English-Chinese Bilingual Book

Hiss! Pop! Boom!
By Tricia Morrissey;
Calligraphy by Kong Lee

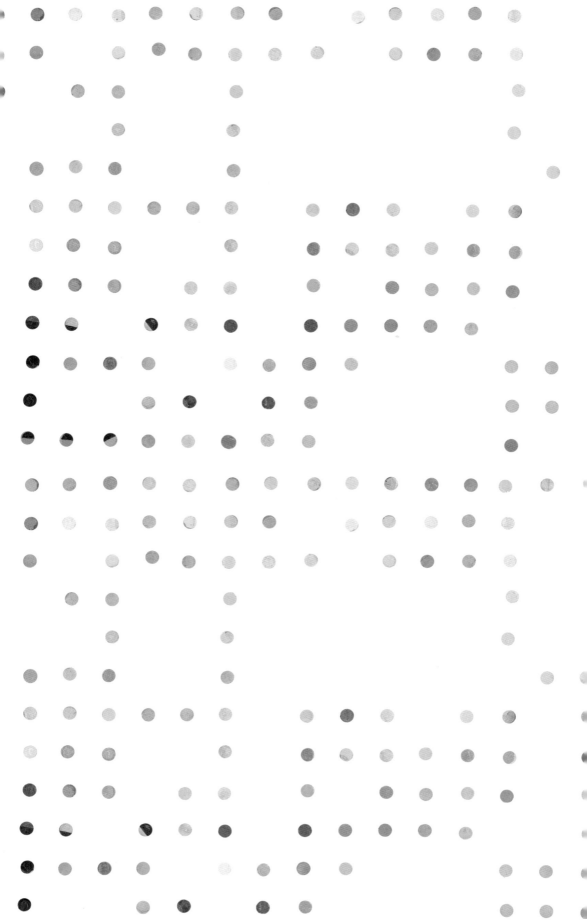